The 122 TURN-OFFS

GW00633308

A CATALOGUE OF
UNNERVING ENCOUNTERS
BY

Kjartan Poskitt & Steven Appleby

GRUB STREET · LONDON

Published by Grub Street
The Basement, 10 Chivalry Road, London SW11 1HT

Copyright © Grub Street 1993
Text Copyright © Kjartan Poskitt 1993
Drawings Copyright © Steven Appleby 1993

The right of Kjartan Poskitt and Steven Appleby to be identified
as the creators of this work has been asserted by them in
accordance with the Copyright, Designs and Patents Act 1988

A catalogue record for this title is available from the British Library

ISBN 0 948817 83 6

Printed and bound by Biddles Ltd, Guildford and King's Lynn

Water repellent skin

Jesus sandle flavoured crisps

Bunk beds on honeymoon

Little Alice playing with a brown
torpedo in the paddling pool

Fishing net tights

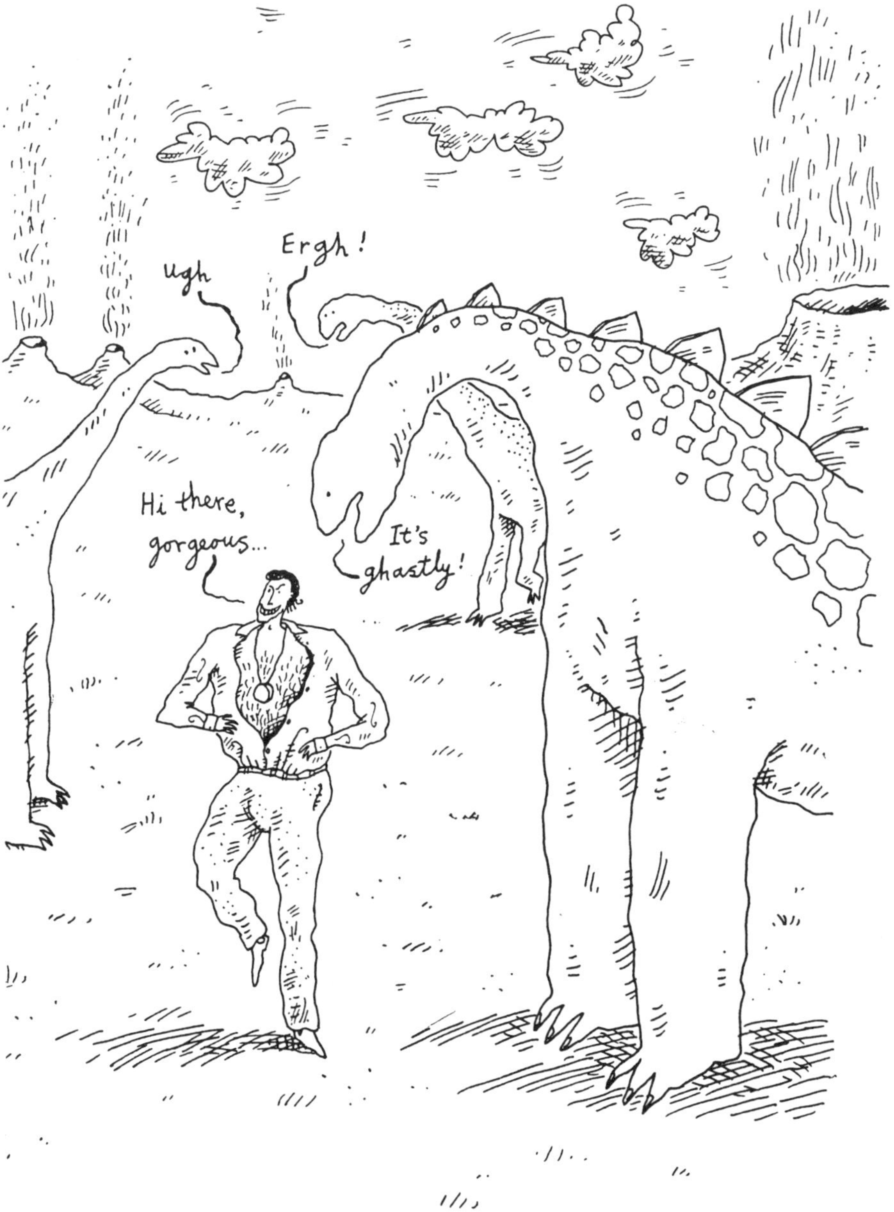
Ugh
Ergh!
Hi there, gorgeous...
It's ghastly!

Premature evolution

The flat next to the dentist

Phwoar...

UGH!

Live patches on the shower curtain

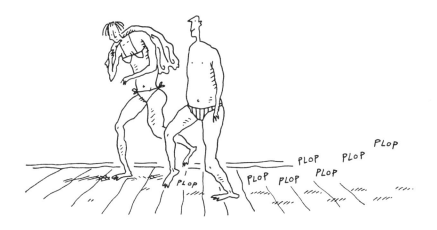

Sucker feet

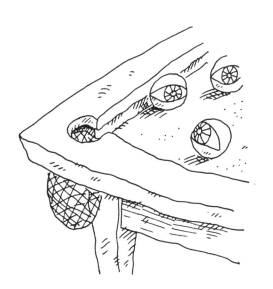

Improvising a game of pool in a glass eye factory

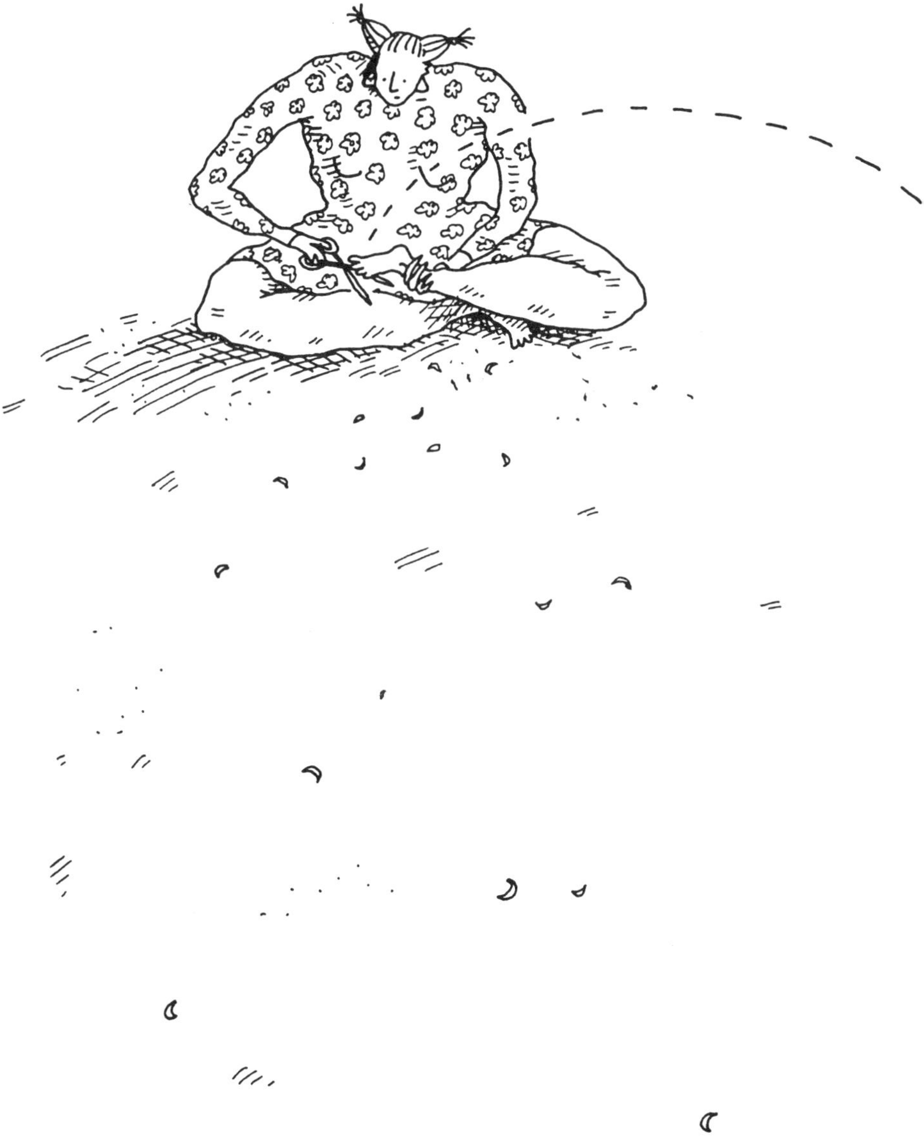

Toenail artillery

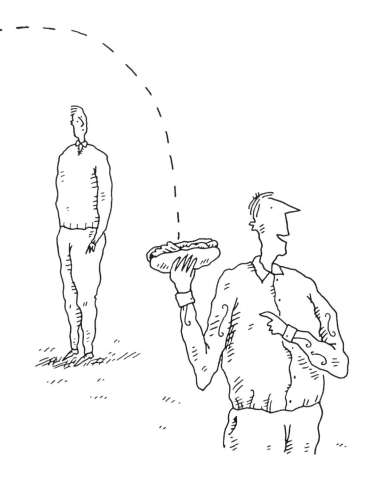

Unexpected protein

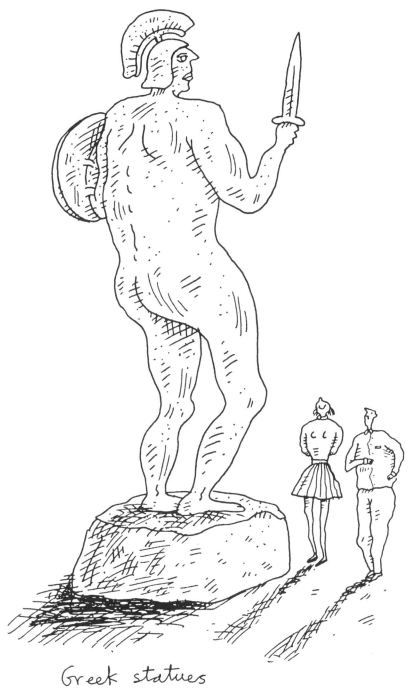

Greek statues

Fish squatters

A sneezing newsreader

Unexpected vending machines

A queue to see a memorial to someone who was nothing else but rich

The Flintstones skinny dipping

Conversation in the next cubicle

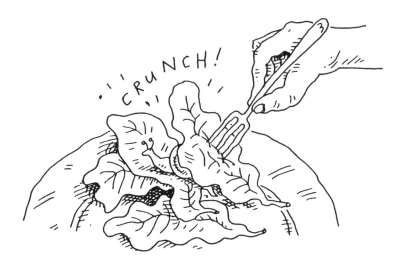

Brittle lettuce

Black underwear which isn't
supposed to be

Valentines addressed to
'The occupier'

A squid-ink pen

A flatulence maestro

Pavement crack enforcement zone

Dogspawn

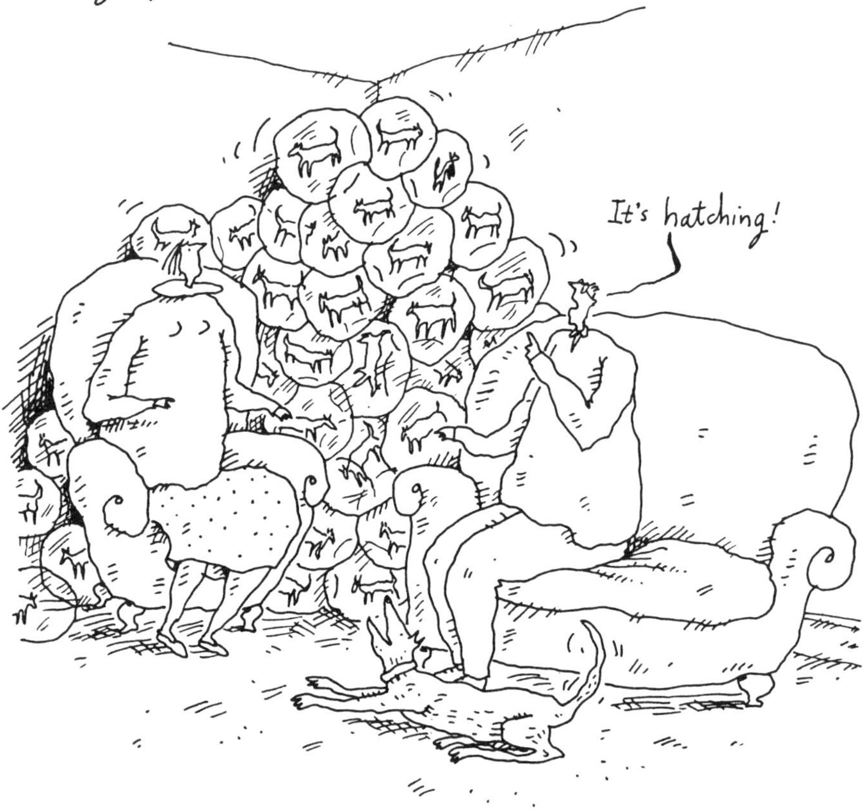
It's hatching!

The over-powered Power Shower

The self-seeking-anti-tank-missile-firing tank

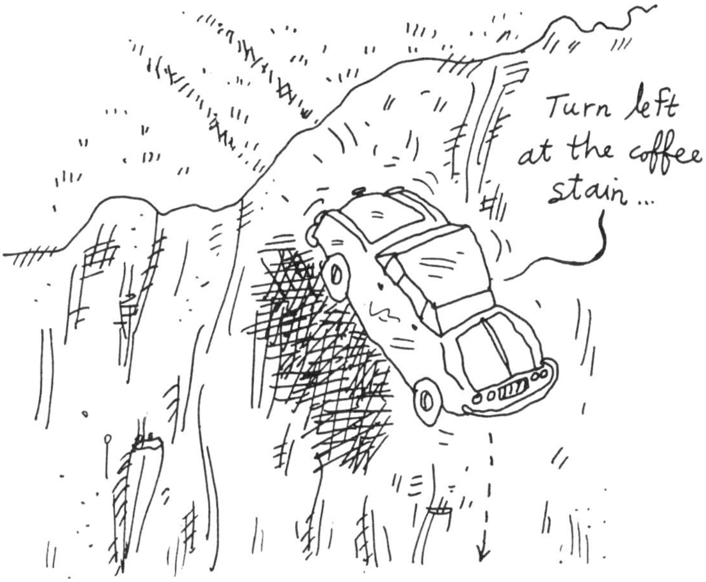
Turn left at the coffee stain...

An old road map

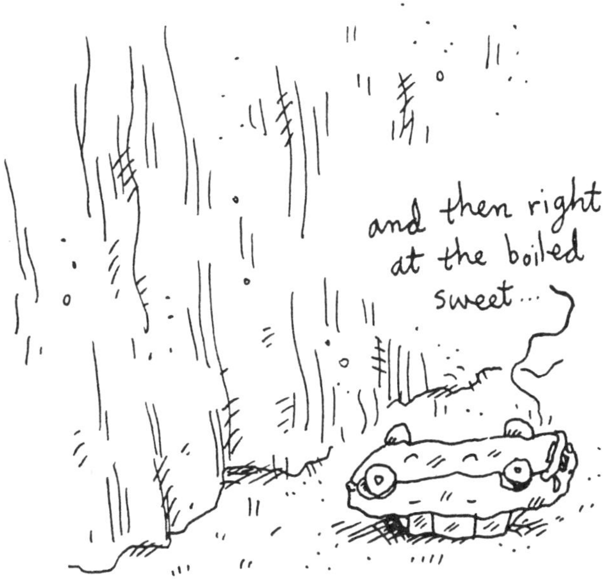
and then right at the boiled sweet...

Using the wrong aerosol

Extra items back from
the laundrette

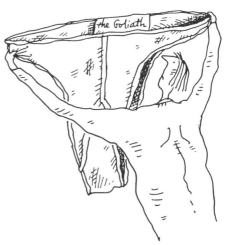

The forgotten grocery bag

Foot-in-mouth disease

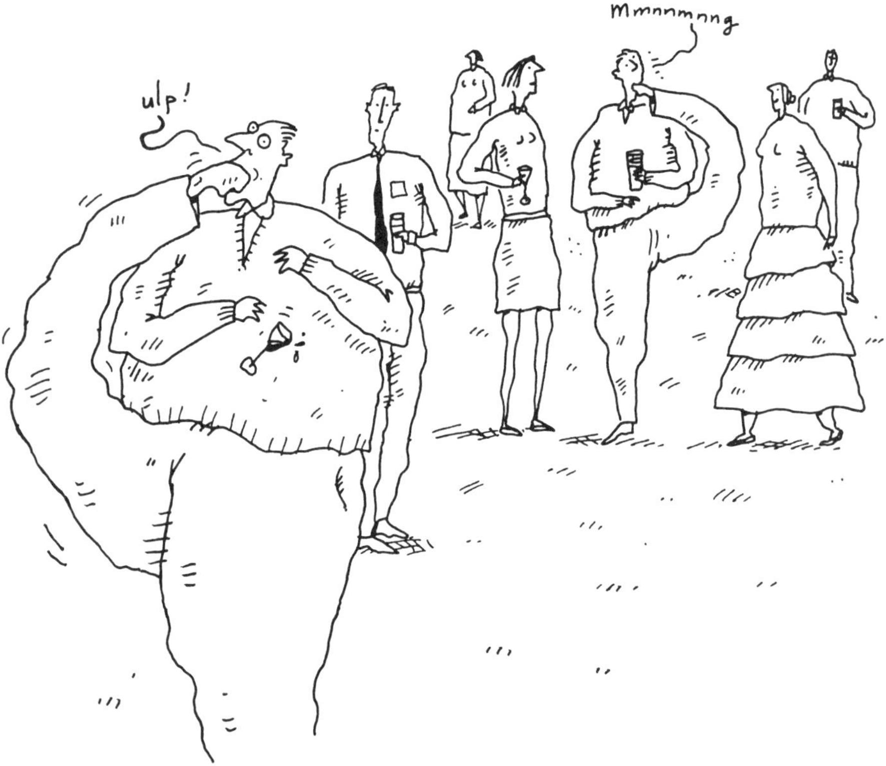
ulp!
Mmnnmnng

Tapeworm bolognaise...

...with spider leg toothpicks

Anonymous tins

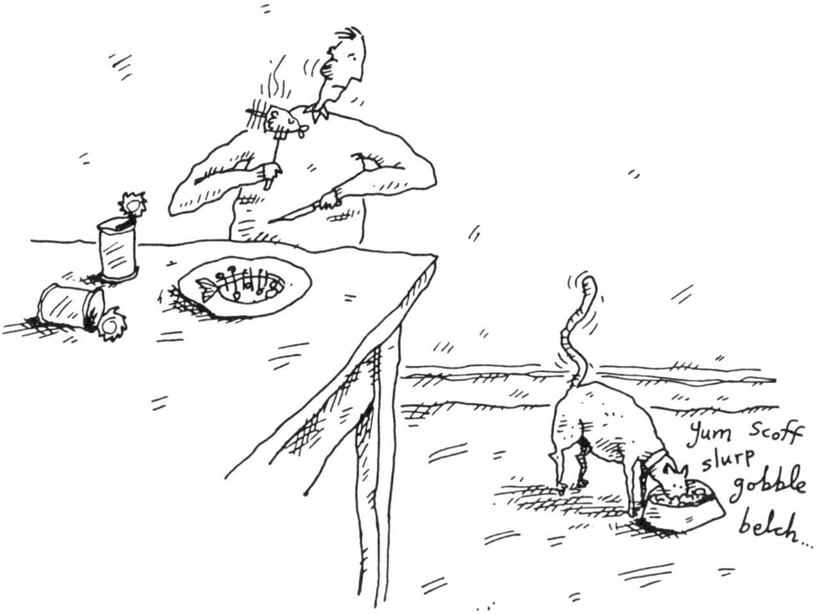
Yum Scoff
slurp
gobble
belch...

Improvised wigs

Baaaa...

Jellyfish and chips

Power dressing

Hors-d'oeuvres that are still twitching

Noisy smoochers

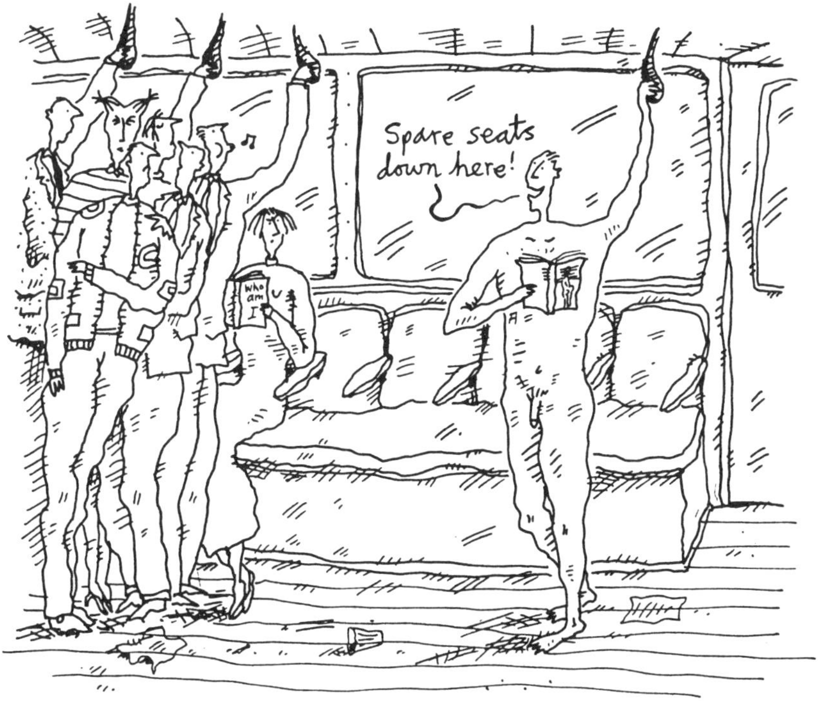
Spare seats down here!
Who am I

Unabashed nudists

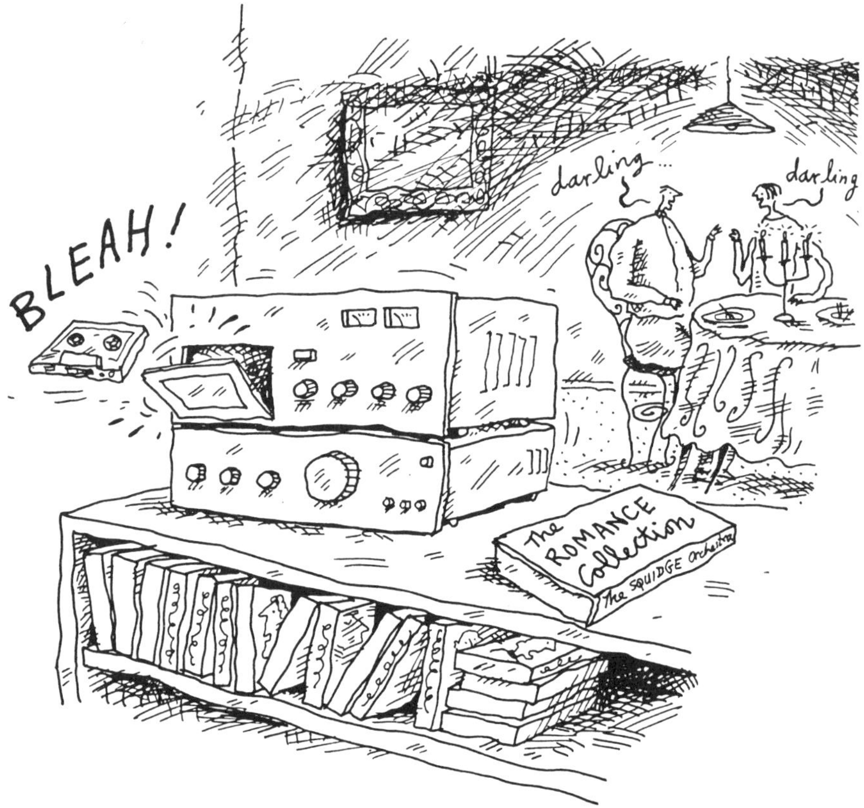
BLEAH!
darling...
darling
The ROMANCE Collection
The SQUIDGE Orchestra

Critical stereo

People who wear dark glasses at night

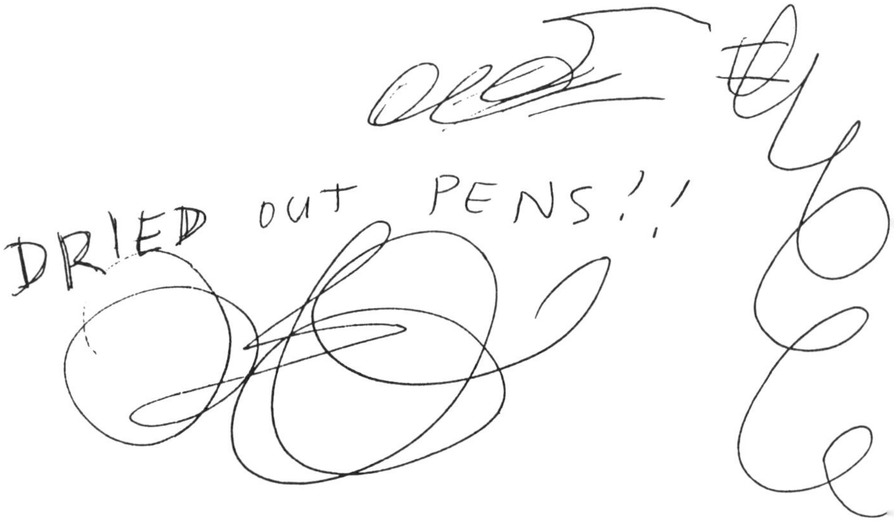
DRIED OUT PENS!!

Hessian sheets

Smelly money

Green meat

Inlaws...

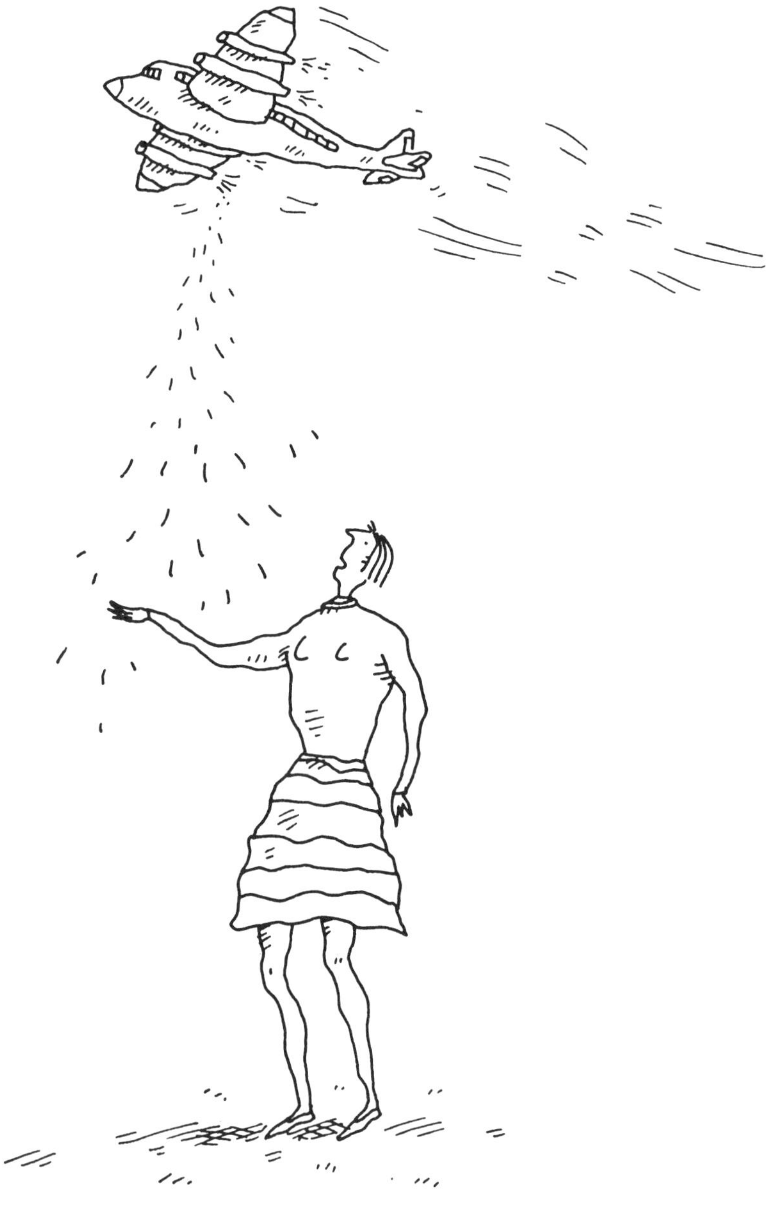

Yellow rain

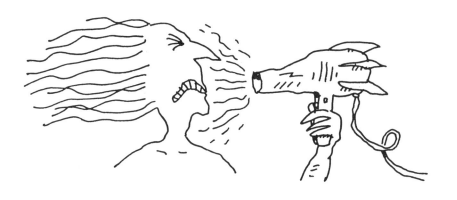

A hairdryer with halitosis

Sunbathing fish

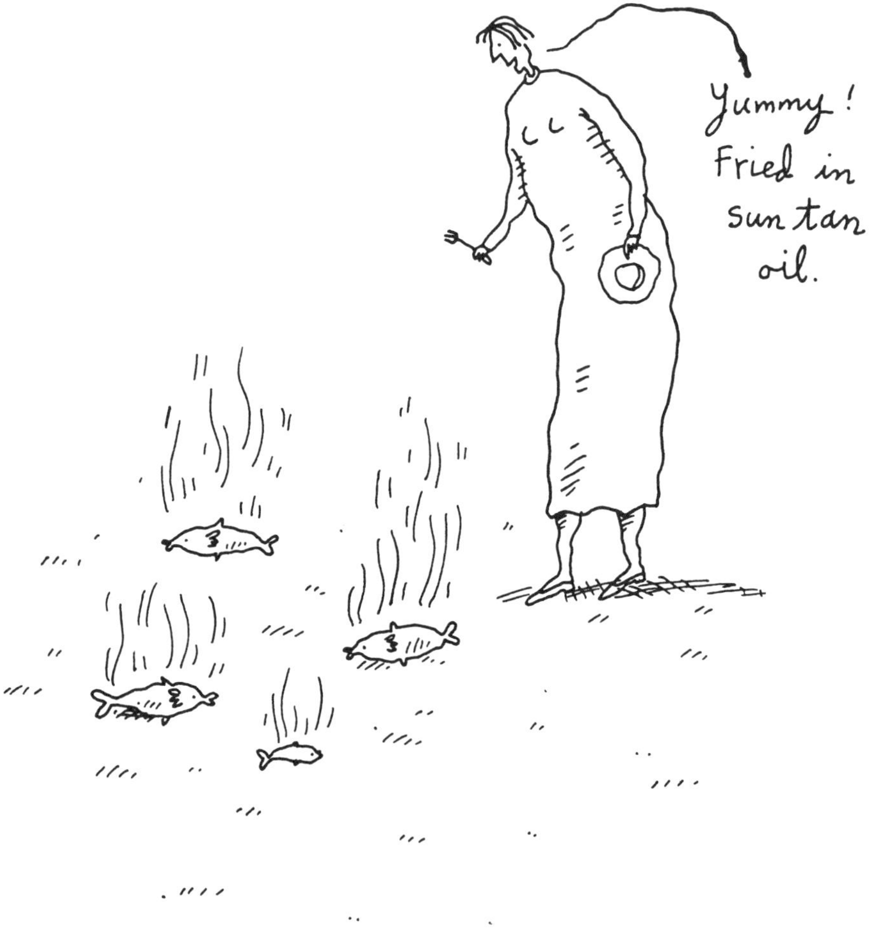
Yummy! Fried in sun tan oil.

Fire's gone out.

The hidden swamp

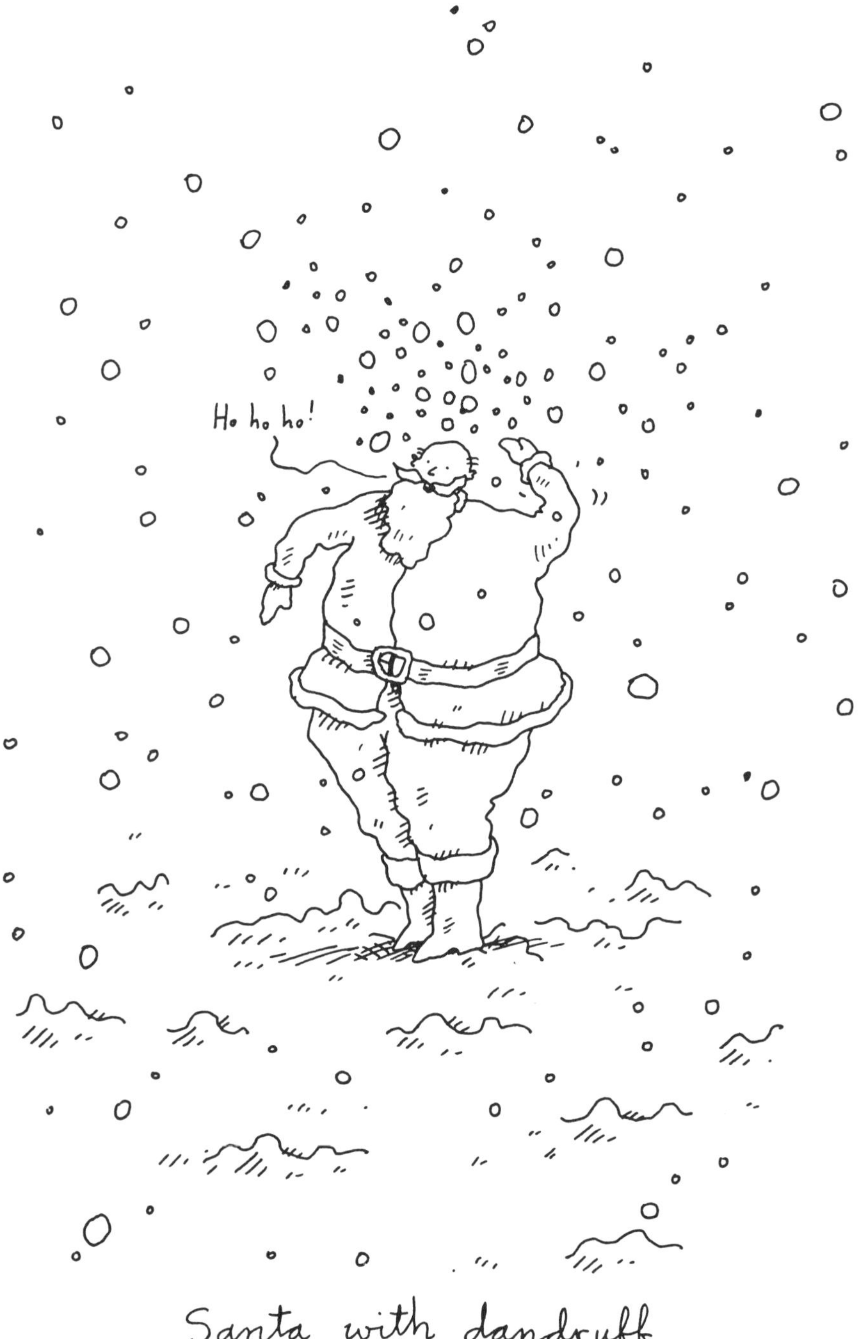
Ho ho ho!

Santa with dandruff

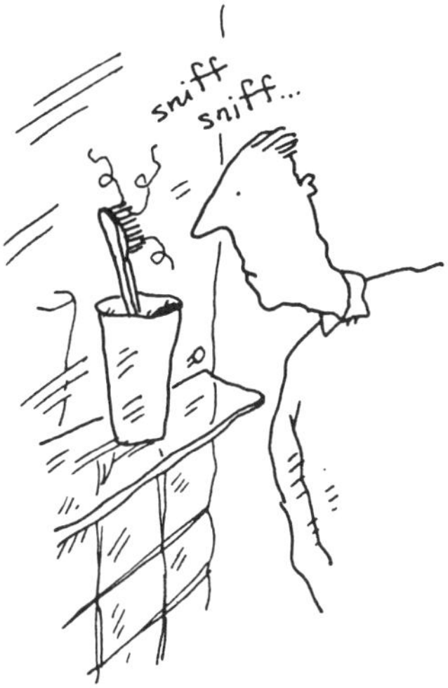
sniff
sniff...

Knowing someone has just used your toothbrush but not knowing what for

Finding the top of the shampoo all alone in your suitcase

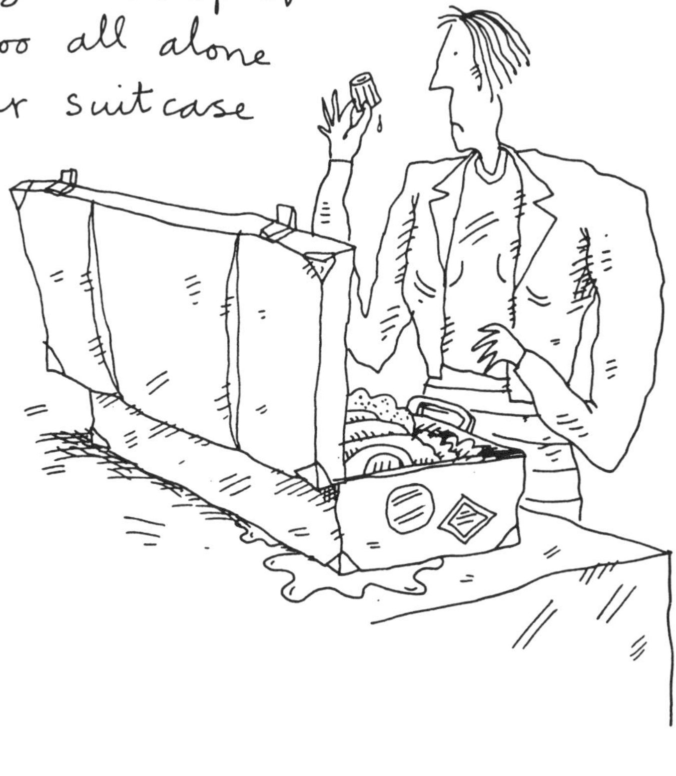

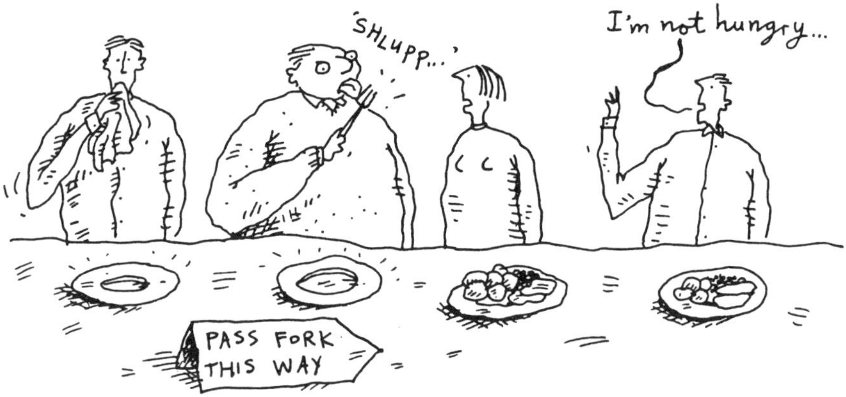
'SHLUPP...'
I'm not hungry...
PASS FORK
THIS WAY

A cutlery shortage

Personally I'd have expected more foreplay.

People who don't realise that "very well, thank you" is the only socially acceptable response to "How are you?"

... and my rash has come back and last week I was coughing up in several colours...

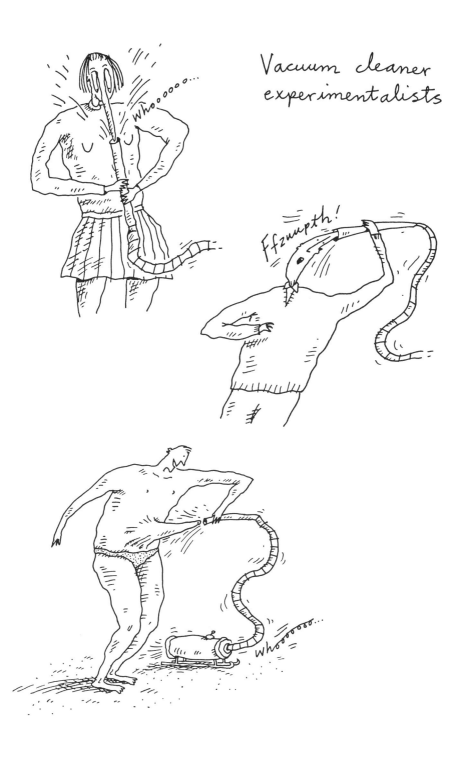

Vacuum cleaner experimentalists

Recognising the voice on a medical phone-in

Chess cheats

People who assume it's okay to slip
their shoes off in your kitchen

Parking meters that only accept
Krugerands

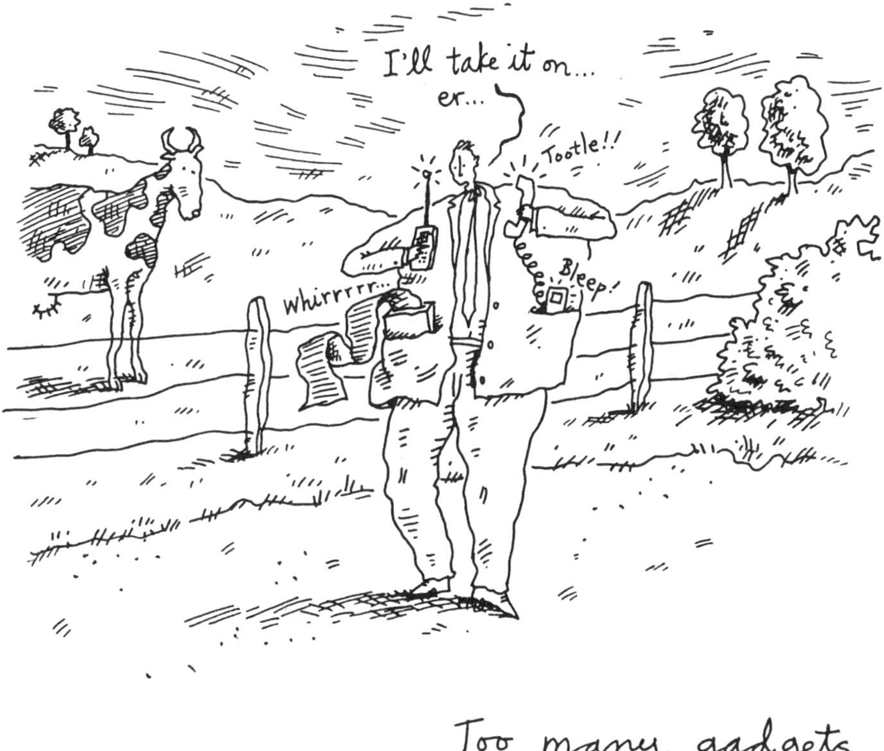
I'll take it on...
er...
Tootle!!
Bleep!
whirrrrr...

Too many gadgets

Other people's bedspring concertos.

Writers who think
they can draw!!

'JUNIOR MISS' vivisectionist set

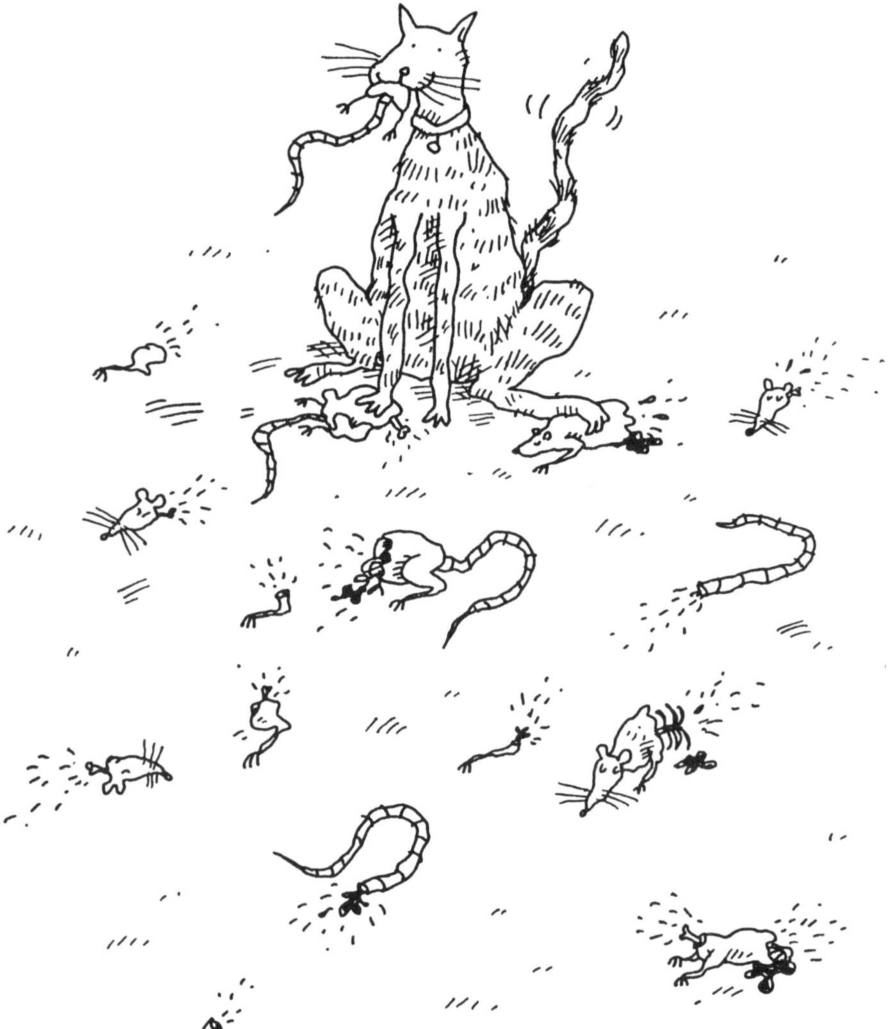

A happy cat

Thin people who say they
need to loose weight

Unsolicited advice...

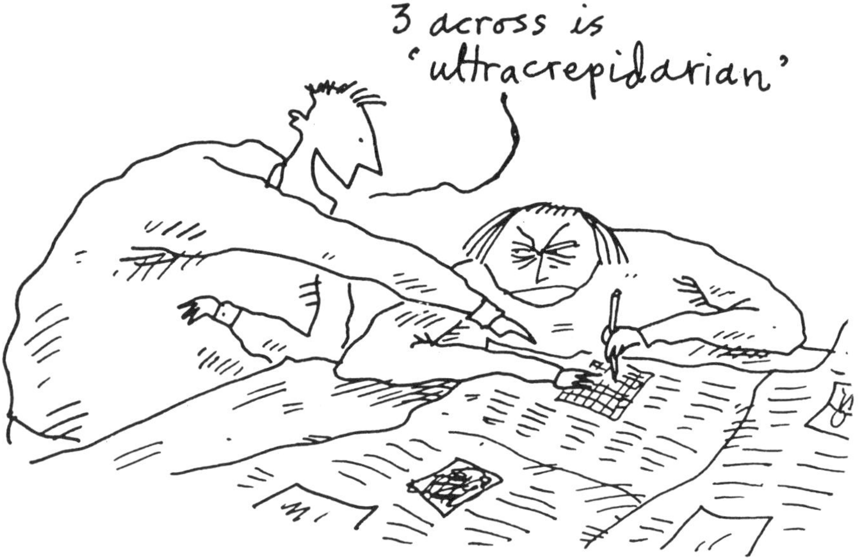
3 across is 'ultracrepidarian'

... and dangerous advice

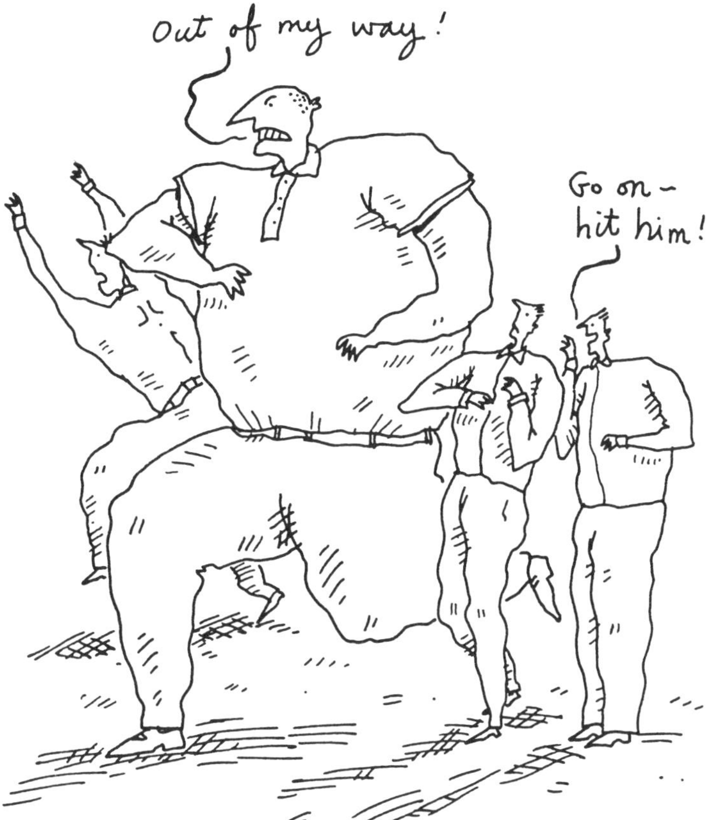
Out of my way!
Go on – hit him!

Self-raising kilt

Running barefoot through a
pubic plantation

Photograph gatecrashers

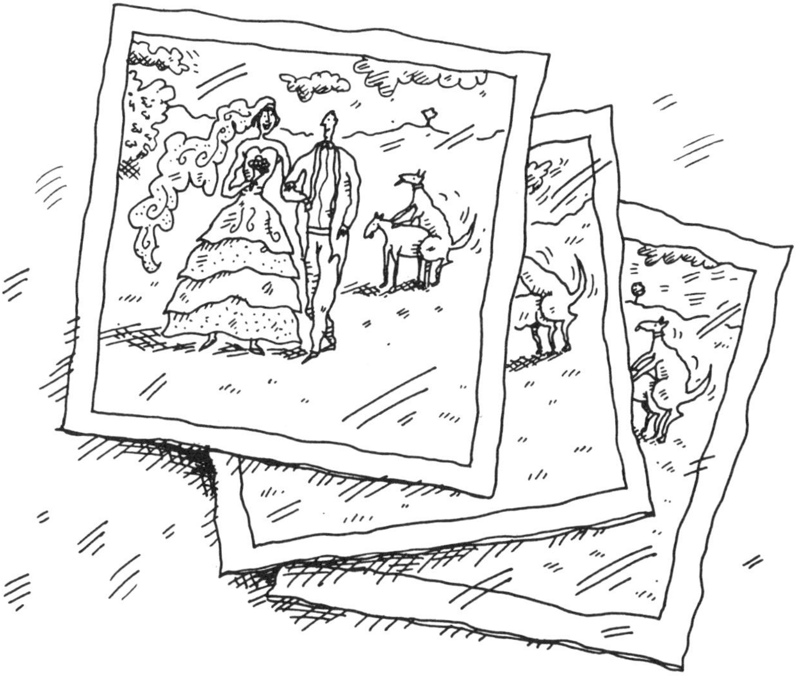

Flat animals

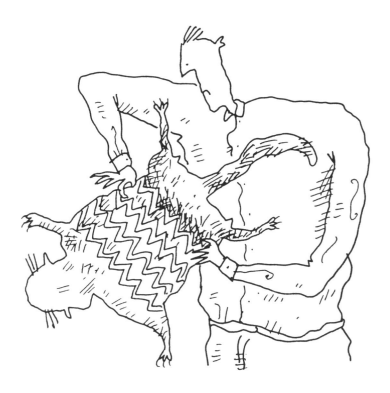

Armpit moths

Unusual relish

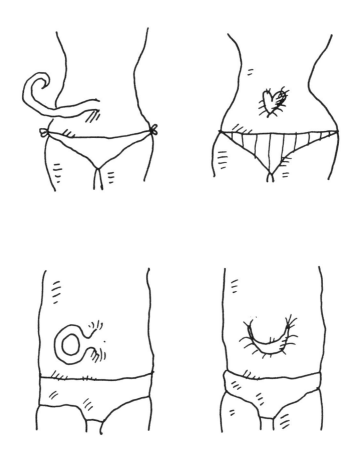

Navel cosmetic surgery

Toilet with job
satisfaction

Oversized brains

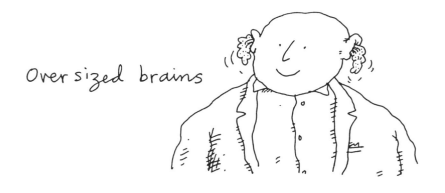

Seeing the magician's assistant
in her dressing room

Sexy legs

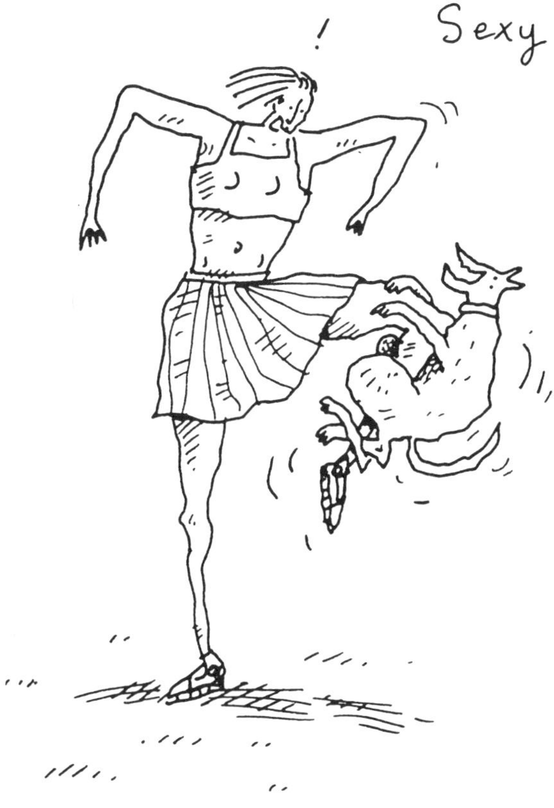
!

Bathroom security cameras

Re-cycled teeth

The pillow spider

People with too many microphones
and not enough to say

People who make you feel
obliged to lie

People who overuse their
favourite expression

Saturated toilet roll

Going Dutch with a glutton

The juice from a rock band's socks

Careless shavers

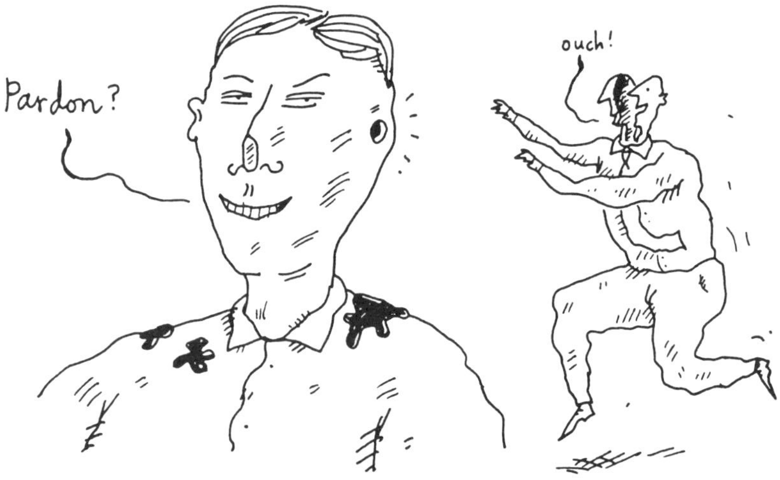
Pardon?
ouch!

Conversational sprinklers

Failing to negotiate the cocktail stick

Glutinous tap water

Spotty mushrooms

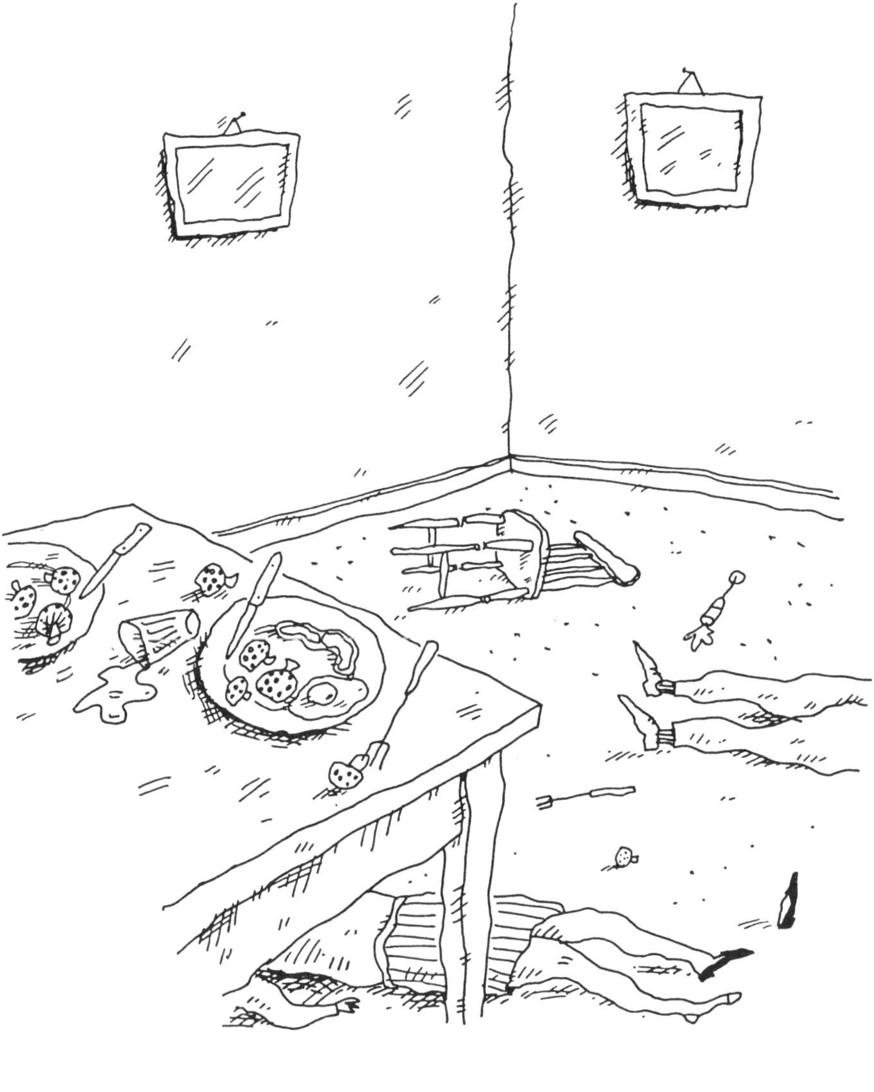

Kebab droppings

The endless eyebrow

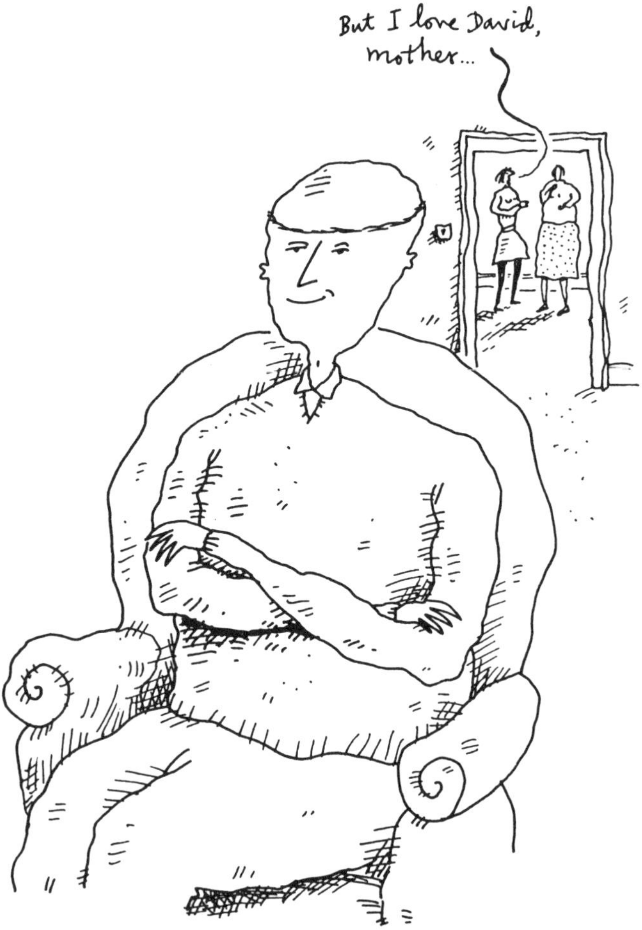
But I love David, mother...

Demonic supermarket trolleys

Being able to tell a man's diet by the contents of his beard

Secret handshakes

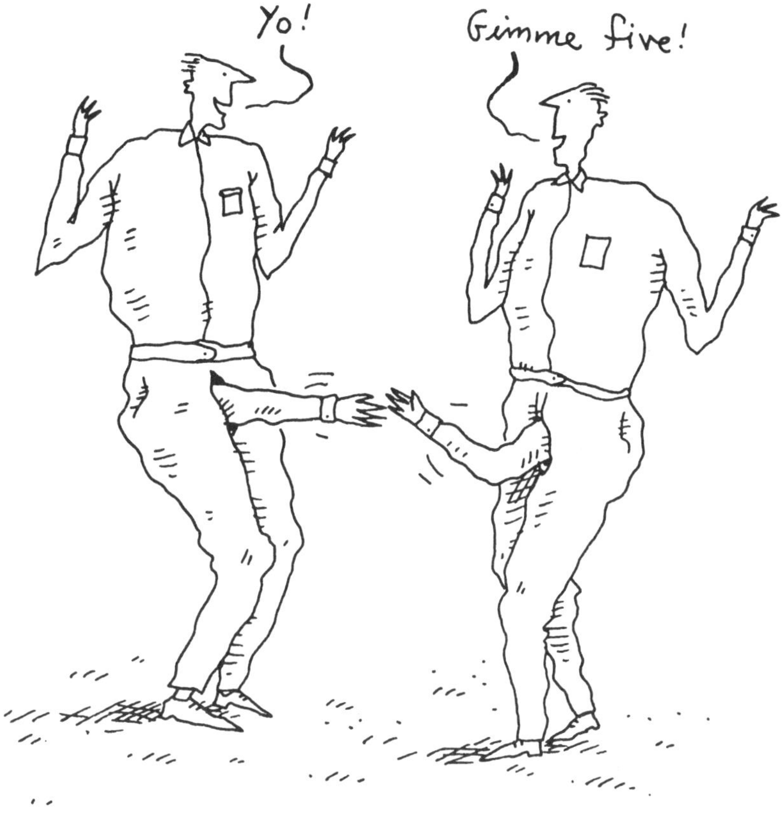
Yo!
Gimme five!

The damp seat in the cinema

Self-chewing gum

Self-bubble blowing too!
CHOMP
GNASH
GUZZLE...

Warm underwear

funny...

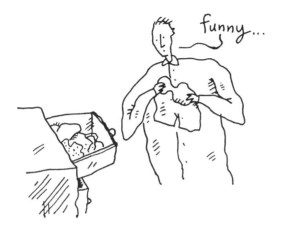

Only just realising that you
caught a thread

Slugman!

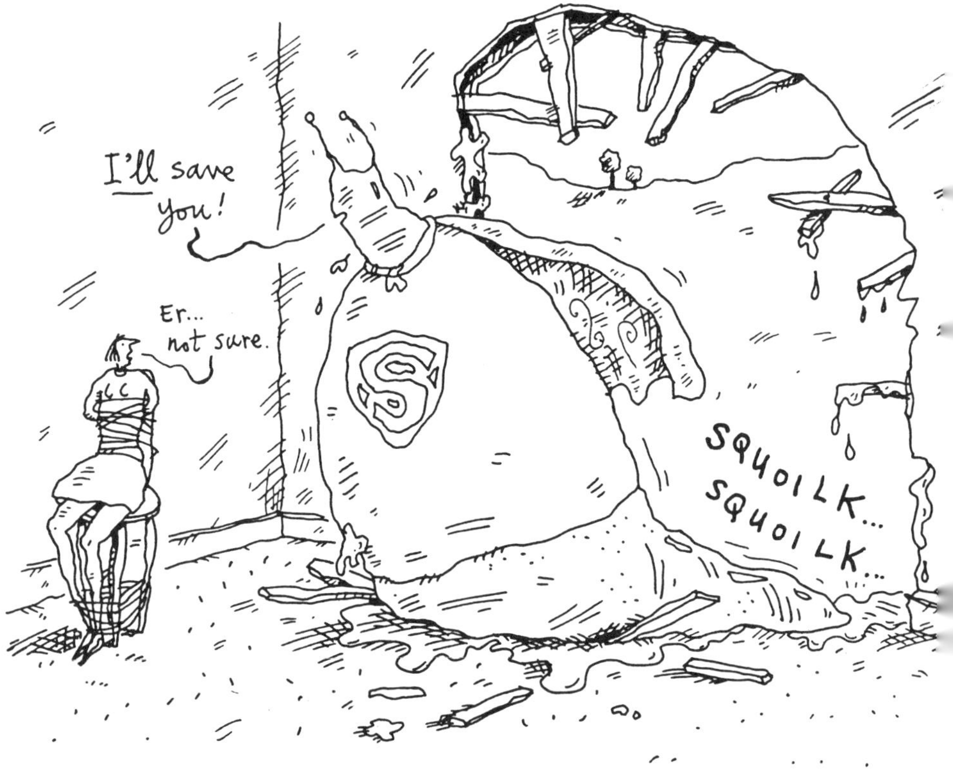
I'll save you!
Er... not sure.
SQUOILK...
SQUOILK...

A stranger's spectacles...

... and his hat

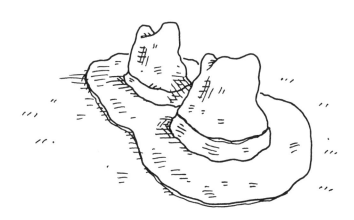

A pet rock that isn't
house trained

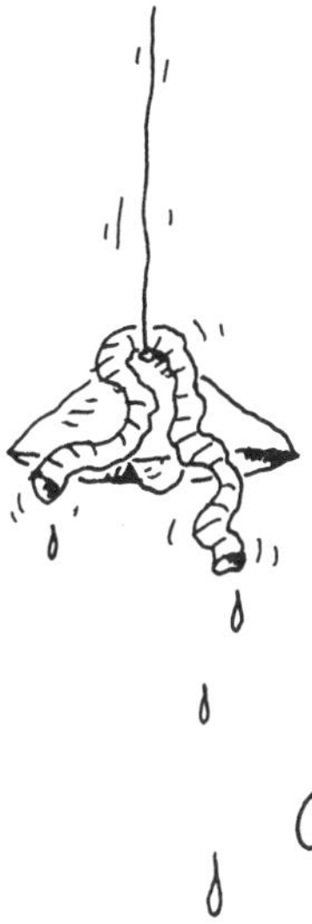

Offal juggling

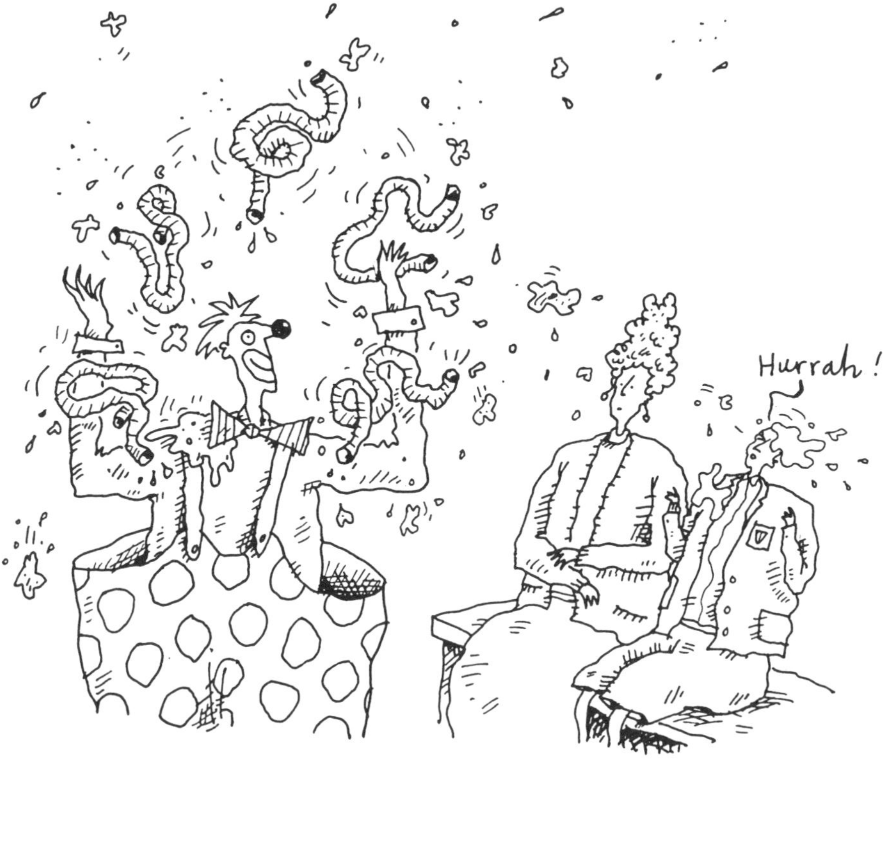
Hurrah!

Illegible prescriptions

Dog with high water pressure

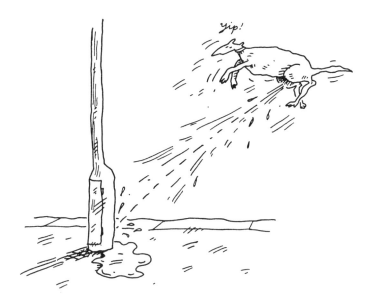

Tongue leeches

An exterior stomach

"...well if you'd seen the cardigan she'd knitted for Henry you'd have laughed, like I said before he's so short and forever losing his contact lenses, in fact last week one fell out while he was hoovering inside the freezer and two days later it turned up in Mrs Prendergast's gin and tonic... of course you might not know them, but they're very big in fish and always slip us a couple of slices of best turbot after church, not that I like turbot that much, well they say it can make your skin go oily, no hang on I'm getting confused, isn't that olives? George can't eat them you know, he says he gets a sudden rash between his toes, I asked him which toes in particular and he said "my two big ones" cheeky, if you come across him you want to watch yourself, mind you he's a demon bowler, or he was until that incident with the Great Dane, but he should have looked before he bent over shouldn't he...."

Wrong number callers who can't be deterred

Nuggets

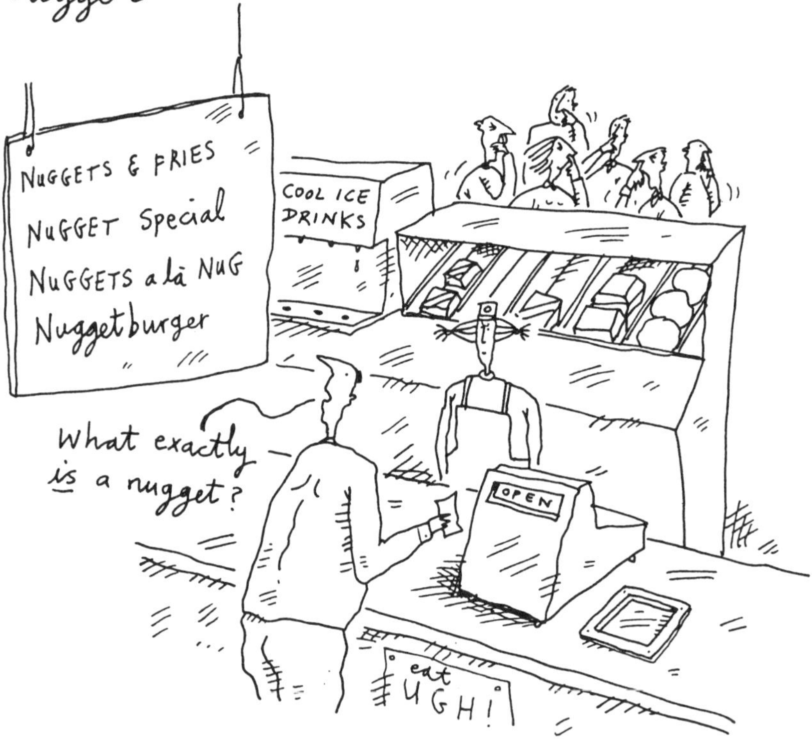

NUGGETS & FRIES
NUGGET Special
NUGGETS a là NUG
Nuggetburger
COOL ICE DRINKS
What exactly is a nugget?
OPEN
eat UGH!

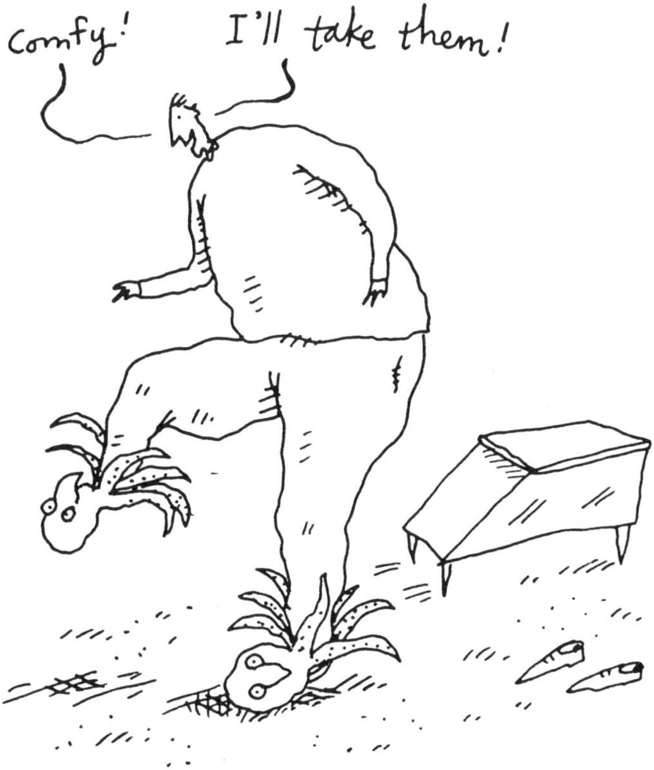
Comfy!
I'll take them!

Octopus skin shoes

High intensity disco lasers

Platted earlobes

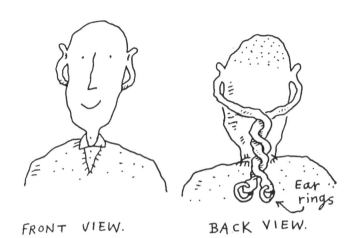

FRONT VIEW.   BACK VIEW.

Ear rings

Carnivores salad

A sudden itch moving towards you

STAND HERE

Unexplained signs

People who assume you like your name shortened

Three nostrils

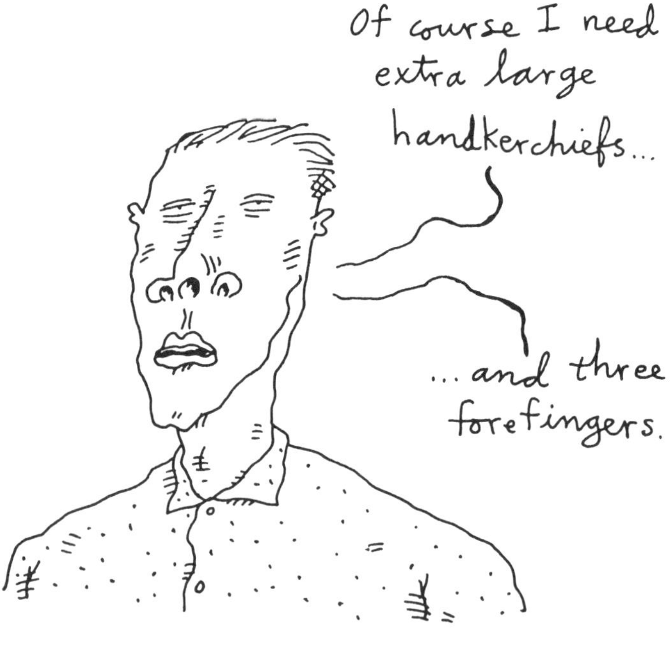
Of course I need extra large handkerchiefs...
...and three forefingers.

Cold feet in bed

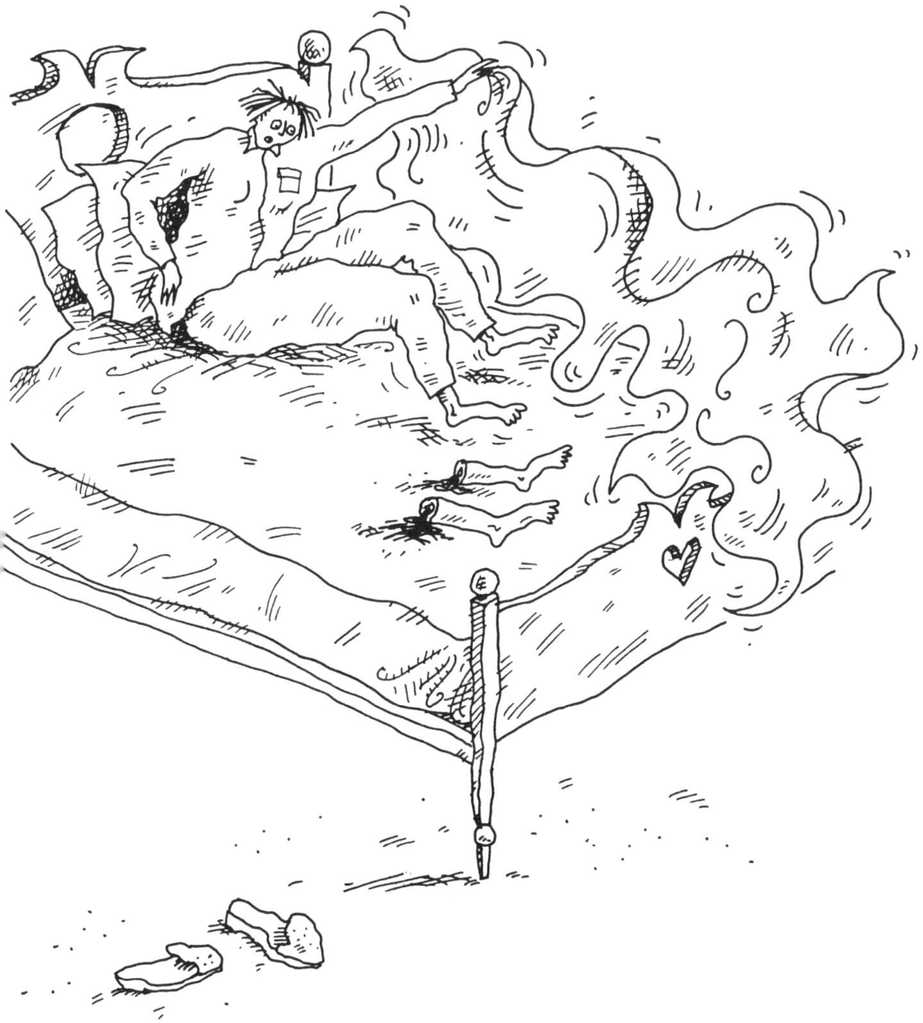

A cheap plug for another book by the same authors